'Though I do not believe
that a plant will spring up
where no seed has been,
I have great faith in a seed.
Convince me that you
have a seed there, and I am
prepared to expect wonders.'

Henry David Thoreau, *Faith in a Seed*

Creative team

Contributors

Images

Editor-in-chief
Carole Bamford

Creative Director
Claudie Dubost

Editorial Director
Imogen Fortes

Contributing Editor
Sophie Richardson

Production Coordinator
Matthew Gorman

Words
Carole Bamford
Leonora Bamford
Alice B-B
Sebastian Cox
Spencer Fung
Katriona Jones
Rhaya Jordan
Satish Kumar
Ben Olsen
Sophie Richardson
Ralph Rugoff
Craig Sams
Jez Taylor
Gelong Thubten
Malika Verma

Recipes
Gaven Fuller
Lydia Lishman

Photography
Alice B-B
Helen Cathcart
Helen Dufresne
Jesse Frohman
Gourab Ganguli
Matthew Gorman
Kris Graves
Lizzie Mayson
Martin Morrell
Prarthna Singh
Sophia Spring
Jerry Thompson

Styling
Linda Berlin
Claudie Dubost
Frankie Unsworth

Illustration
Hugo Guinness
Blandine Pannequin
Paula Troxler

Printed in the United
Kingdom at
Wood Mitchell Printers
on 100% recycled paper
using vegetable inks.

Cover photography by
Martin Morrell

@seed_magazine

Dear Reader,

We find ourselves in a very different climate to the one in which we had hoped to be launching this issue of our magazine and as a team we wanted you to know that *Seed* had been sent to the printers before the onset of the global pandemic.

You will therefore find reference to events, such as the exhibition by Spencer Fung featured on the cover, which have sadly been postponed; or others, such as the Hayward Gallery's *Among the Trees* that you can now visit virtually, thanks to an online tour accompanied by the gallery's director.

We hope that the magazine's content will offer you a little joy and hope in these times – perhaps in the form of escapism or inspiration, as well as ways to calm your mind and nourish yourself both physically and mentally. We are extremely grateful to you for your support, and wish you peace and safety and the courage to weather this storm.

Carole Bamford, Editor-in-chief

Contents

Seed likes

A BOOK

'The Wisdom of No Escape'
by Pema Chödrön

|

A PLACE

Villa Noailles, Hyères, France
Go for the International Festival of Fashion

|

A POEM

'Why I Wake Early'
Mary Oliver

|

A TABLE

Silo
Hackney Wick, London

|

AN EXHIBITION

The Natural Room
Sarah Myerscough
at 103 Pimlico Road, London

Editor's letter

PORTRAIT Martin Morrell

Since we published our first volume of *Seed* last autumn, I have been hugely inspired and encouraged to watch the speed with which the landscape around sustainable living is evolving. There have been trailblazing innovations in the sector – from the rise in online platforms offering clothes to rent, to the pioneering fabrics being engineered from recycled plastics, and the pledges from prominent organisations offering to drastically cut their waste or environmental footprint. The creativity and appetite for change makes me excited and gives me great hope.

Yet in spite of the enormous strides forward, there are daily and potent signs of the state of the crisis we are facing. Last year the world witnessed environmental disaster on a colossal scale, watching in desperation as bushfires ravaged Australia's landscapes and wildlife, taking human lives and homes, and wiping out species, biodiversity and natural habitat. The events were a tragic reminder of the urgency with which we still need to act.

With that in mind, this issue of *Seed* is devoted to the individuals and organisations that are choosing to help redress the wrongdoings of the past both vocally and visibly. We celebrate the artists and craftspeople working to highlight the plight of the planet, regenerate its resources or use their voice and their craft to fight against social or ecological injustice. Our writers applaud the efforts of the enterprises helping to clean our skies by turning to alternative forms of energy or choosing to farm in a way that removes the polluting gases from the atmosphere. And we consider one of nature's most majestic forms – the tree and the vital role that the lungs of our planet have in helping to heal its wounds.

I hope that volume two will remind you of the responsibility we each have to work in harmony with nature and offer you inspiring ways to play your own part in fighting to change the planet's future.

– Carole Bamford

IN CONVERSATION WITH
MAYA LIN

WORDS Carole Bamford
PHOTOGRAPHY Jesse Frohman, Kris Graves, Jerry Thompson

Maya Lin is an artist, architect, designer and environmental activist who sees and interprets the natural world through art, science, politics and history. Lin's design for the *Vietnam Veterans Memorial* in Washington, DC catapulted her on to the international stage in 1981. Since then, she has established a career in both art and architecture while maintaining a strong interest in works that reflect on significant socio-political movements of our time (*The Civil Rights Memorial,* and the *Women's Table* at Yale University). Lin's art explores how we experience and relate to nature and asks the viewer to reconsider our treatment of the environment at a time when it is crucial to do so. With the final work in the memorial series, *What is Missing?*, Lin is reinventing the concept of the medium with a cross-platform, global memorial to the planet that calls attention to the crisis surrounding biodiversity and habitat loss and showcases how we can balance our needs with the needs of the planet.

Where does your interest in, and concern for, nature and our relationship with it stem from?

My childhood home was down a very long, spooky driveway, surrounded by woods, and three separate streams flowed down the hills around it. As a child, if I wasn't making art or studying (I was very bookish), I would be outdoors playing with my brother. I would sit on the front lawn, completely still until I could get a rabbit to come close to me, or hand-feed racoons. I was very connected to being in nature.

I was born in 1959 so the Vietnam War and civil rights movement were the backdrop to my impressionable years: the Clean Air, Clean Water and Endangered Species Acts were all coming into play in America in the early 1970s when I was in high school. And I couldn't figure out how one species had a right to overrun the planet. My high school days were spent in this tiny town in Athens, Ohio sitting in the parking lot of the grocery store with a petition to boycott Japanese products to save the whales or prevent the use of steel animal traps. My plan was to study animal behaviour in college and then become a field zoologist. My parents couldn't figure out where I got it from but I think I just had an innate sensibility.

What changed? What led to the move into art and architecture?

I studied architecture at Yale in the end because when I arrived my advisor was a science advisor and he explained that studying animal behaviour at Yale is neurologically based and involved vivisection – and I just couldn't do that. I figured architecture would be this perfect blend of art, maths and science. It took me getting through grad school to realise that I was an artist; I had been making art my entire childhood (my father had been Dean of Fine Arts at Ohio University).

Through your work you're committed to raising awareness of the environmental concerns of our time. How do you feel an artist can address these in ways that other people can't?

I have always believed that art is a very personal endeavour. I call it the selfish art, because each artist has to find their voice. I've felt that through my art I'm going to show you things about the natural world that you might not be thinking of – I present new ways of looking at a river or mountain, say, but I do not try to preach. I want each person to discover and relate to each artwork. Whereas I let the memorial *What is Missing?* become completely prescriptive. I've divided myself

between my art and my memorials, so that the memorials teach you about history. The memorials are never about loss, per se; they are about looking at our past honestly. How can we learn from our past to shape a different future? The first one [the *Vietnam Veterans Memorial*] is about war – we have to face the high price of war. Maybe it's necessary, maybe it's not; but never forget that there is an unbelievable cost and always weigh that out. The memorials are teaching tools; all but *What is Missing?* stay neutral, presenting history's truth and letting the viewer come to their own conclusions.

But *What is Missing?* focuses on species loss and links it to climate change by showing how much of our emissions are caused by land degradation, loss and land use change. For the first time, I am being very solutions-based and prescriptive. Climate change poses an existential threat to mankind, to the planet and to all the species we share it with. We are at a critical point in time and I want to emphasise how important nature-based solutions could be in significantly reducing emissions (through restorative agriculture, reforming ranching practices and sustainable forestry practices), restoring our degraded landscapes and protecting more forests, grasslands and wetlands. *What is Missing?* shows you what we are losing but also focuses on the solutions – both the choices we can each make, as well as the larger macro solutions that are realisable today.

'Folding the Hudson', 2018; Photograph: Kris Graves, courtesy of Pace Gallery

2°|4°, 2018;
Photograph: Kris Graves,
courtesy of Pace Gallery

'The memorials are teaching tools; all but *What is Missing?* stay neutral, presenting history's truth and letting the viewer come to their own conclusions.'

Do you feel a responsibility to confront these questions and to use them as themes in your art?

I do. Look at my series about river waterway systems: we never think of our rivers; other than knowing that we know we live on that river. And we almost never think about what's downstream from us. But we do care what's upstream from us if someone happens to be dumping their raw sewage in it. I look at our waterways and how easy it would be to create watershed protection, to ensure that our waters stays clean. It's complex but it's within our reach and we know the consequences.

I created a permanent piece for the New Orleans Museum of Art called *Folding the Mississippi* which shows the Mississippi watershed whose lifeblood has been completely poisoned by fertilisers. It replicates the river using recycled industrial glass marbles that wind across the wall and the ceiling and the green marbles catch and reflect the light. It's trying to make you understand an entire complex river system as a beautiful singularity.

For the Hudson River Museum, I created an entire site-specific exhibition around pieces focusing on the Hudson and its surrounding waterways. *2°|4°* shows what happens to Manhattan if temperatures rise by 2 degrees and what happens if they get 4 degrees warmer. People don't understand what's really happening. I read this great book recently – *The Uninhabitable Earth* – in which the author, David Wallace- Wells, tells us that things are much worse that we think. He goes on to say, we've 30 years to turn this around. I have too many friends of my generation who believe that our kids will sort this out. We got ourselves into this mess and if we care about the next generation we have to start moving.

So that's how it started in me; I went with the lifeblood of the planet, which is water: I'm very drawn to water, but now I'm equally drawn to the earth.

The choice to use technology and digital media for *What is Missing?* – was that a very deliberate choice because of the footprint?

Yes it was. It's also that I'm an artist who works in series. So even though I start with the *Vietnam Veterans Memorial* and everyone says it's this wall plopped into the earth, it's a geode; you've cut the earth and you've polished it and the names are the object. So the logical culmination for the memorials series is one that would be pure data: information and history.

If we do something on the web it's on a black background because you use less energy; if it's something printed it's always on white because you use less ink. I try not to print much and to create something that is shared by all and could go anywhere. The work always starts with, 'can we convey the message in a minimal way?' I've come a long way from the very first *Wave Field*, which I

want to revisit with the University of Michigan to ensure that it's organic. Whereas the piece I've just put in at Princeton – *The Princeton Line*, an earth drawing for their new arts campus, has been organic from the beginning. When the piece got set in, we installed a hidden drip irrigation system so we've tried to minimise our water usage. And once it's up and running I want it to go brown and dormant at times. I am keen on on utilising sustainable landscape practices – using organic soils and fertilisers, incorporating native and hardy grasses and trying to minimise water usage and dark sky lighting.

The *Vietnam Veterans Memorial* went on to become one of the most recognisable sculptures in the world, and heralded a sea change for memorial design, but as an artist I wonder if that association with a particular piece can sometimes feel like a burden or a recognition from which you want to break free?

I think when I first did it, for my sake, I ignored it, and chose to continue my education, so I enrolled on and completed my master's degree in architecture. For three years I just worked on architecture. But my professors were quite concerned because they couldn't figure out why this person with the perfect opportunity was just rebelling. I was also drifting over to the art department and beginning to make art again.

It took almost a decade before people would recognise or comment on my

other work. It took me almost 10 years to do enough artworks – through which I was beginning to find my voice – in order for the trained art or architecture world to see me as what I am, which is maybe a hybrid. Once I figured out what my voice was, which is very much being in love with and caring about the environment, I began to feel more confident as a person and as an artist.

We like specialisation – as a population we like to silo. So if you're interdisciplinary, people have a much harder time seeing what you're doing. Forty years later people finally understand this middle path. I love art and architecture and I love the differences between them.

What is Missing?* is described as a global memorial to the planet. It is both a wake-up call and a didactic piece. I wondered whether you are hoping to evoke a very specific reaction in your viewer?

It is a call to action. This year we are completing the first part of *Greenprint*, a section of the *What is Missing?* site that shows you plausible future scenarios for our planet. Its aim is to try to show you what the world could look like if we reform our forestry, ranching or agricultural practices and how by altering our way of life we can help protect species and reduce climate change emissions. For example, if we practise regenerative agriculture, we can absorb almost 40 per cent of all carbon emissions; this is what happens if we

'Storm King Wavefield', 2009; Photograph: Jerry Thompson

all eat 20 per cent less meat… I want to highlight these issues in an interactive mapping experiment to which you can then ratchet your choices to see how they can help increase carbon reductions and restore more habitat.

Because if you put it in perspective, it's 1.3 billion of us that are devouring the world's resources. We could say that there are just too many people in the world, but if we look at how different countries live in terms of resource consumption, how many Americans could live on the planet – only 1.3 billion. We're the consumers and we need to change the way we are overtaxing the world's resources.

What we're trying to do with *Greenprint* is to take all this data – this very complex, dense data and simplify it into infographics, showing 'what if' scenarios that help demonstrate how we could solve climate change emissions and save species by protecting and restoring habitats. We could solve the environmental problems tomorrow. We could reform agriculture by shifting the subsidies that are going to the big industrial practices that are causing carbon to go into the atmosphere. We could transform that, and all of a sudden agriculture goes from being a carbon loss – a carbon emitter – to being a complete carbon sink and we feed a billion more people. *What is Missing?* also showcases successful best practices around the world – in terms of transit, renewables, waste and recycling – helping people to realise

that these solutions are in practice right now – let's just scale them. It's within our grasp. It's something we can all do. If the World Economic Forum says it would take US$700 billion annually to curb climate emissions, we show you what we currently spend worldwide on some things, such as cigarettes (US$681 bn), weight loss (US$385 bn) and bottled water ($400 bn). Let's spend that money to ensure a safe and sustainable future for the next generation. We can blame the oil and gas industries; we can blame China, but there's a high price to cheap goods: we buy 50 per cent of all goods made in China. We have to start thinking about what we're buying. We're all guilty and therefore we all need to do much more.

I've made a promise to myself, for example, that by this time next year, I will have completely neutralised my family's carbon footprint – we've reforested some of our land, but I also want to instal sufficient solar panels in Colorado, where the sunlight is abundant to help achieve net zero emissions for me and my family. Right now I offset my carbon footprint in flights every year, but I want to cut that travel footprint in half at least. I'm really committed but I think we all need to look at what we're doing: what we're buying, how we are travelling. Everything we do – what we eat, what we wear, what we buy and what we throw away – can either help the environment or hurt the environment. Make your choices wisely.

www.whatismissing.net

AMONG THE TREES

WORDS Ralph Rugoff

The tree is an icon of strength and stability, and yet it was not until the twentieth century that its form and symbolism was truly celebrated in art.

The Hayward Gallery in London is exploring the resurgence of trees in contemporary art through an exhibition that not only celebrates the beauty of the tree, but also urges us to consider the essential role that trees and forests play in our lives and psyche.

In an excerpt from the exhibition's catalogue, gallery director Ralph Rugoff shares his motivation for curating the show, which is timed to coincide with the 50th anniversary of World Earth Day.

Approximately 50 years ago, coinciding with the rise of the modern environmental movement, the subject of trees emerged as a motif in works by some of the most adventurous and influential artists of the time.

In the years since, this engagement with trees has grown into a rich vein of contemporary art to which artists working in diverse media and different parts of the world have contributed. While their art draws on the visually arresting character of trees – including their complex spatial and architectural forms – their works convey much more than mere descriptive facts. They invite us to reimagine our relationships with trees and forests as both symbols and living organisms that have helped to shape human civilisation

and continue to play an indispensable role in our lives and imaginations.

Among the Trees gathers together works by more than 30 artists who reconfigure traditional genres and develop new ways of representing trees in order to shift our conventional perceptions and understanding. It surveys a remarkably expansive artistic terrain, encompassing a wide range of approaches and media whilst reflecting on myriad aspects of its universally-recognised, yet still little-understood subject.

Trees provide a point of departure for artists concerned with upending our anthropomorphic perspectives or with confronting us with images that conjure alternative measures of time.

Luisa Lambri 52 53
Untitled (Palácio da Indústria #01), 2003.
Lambda print mounted to acrylic.
© Luisa Lambri 2020. Courtesy the artist

Myoung Ho Lee, Tree... #2, 2012. Ink on Paper, 104 x 152 cm
© the artist 2020. Courtesy Myoung Ho Lee and Gallery Hyundai

Still other artists explore the blurring lines between our concept of nature and culture or seek to prompt reflection on forests as systems characterised by complexity, growth and connectivity, chiming with recent scientific discoveries about the 'wood wide web' – the network of underground roots, fungi and bacteria that connects forest organisms in symbiotic relationships.

Most of the works included in the exhibition do not explicitly raise ecological concerns, yet many almost inevitably bring to mind the vulnerability and precarity of trees and forests in what has been called the Anthropocene era.

According to a 2015 study published in the journal *Nature*, approximately 46 per cent of the world's forests have disappeared since humans began chopping down trees. At present rates of deforestation, there will be no more trees on the planet in 600 years.

It is my hope that *Among the Trees* can provide an inspiring range of perspectives and instil a renewed sense of appreciation for the crucial place that trees occupy in our shared world.

Excerpt from *Among the Trees* catalogue foreword (Hayward Publishing) by Ralph Rugoff, director of the Hayward Gallery.

*'Among the Trees' runs until 17 May
at the Hayward Gallery.
www.southbankcentre.co.uk*

A BREATH
OF FRESH AIR

Harnessing green hydrogen energy might be our most realistic chance of improving air quality – with a host of pioneering enterprises leading the charge.

WORDS Ben Olsen
PHOTOGRAPHY Martin Morrell
ILLUSTRATION Blandine Pannequin

Pursuing alternative, zero-emission fuels remains our best hope for a healthier future

Cleaning up our dirty air has emerged as one of humanity's most pressing concerns. The more familiar we are with the dangerous particles we inhale and their harmful effects, the higher a priority it becomes for our decision makers. In London alone, two million people live with illegal levels of air pollution, something it is hoped the recent introduction of an ultra-low-emission zone will do plenty to improve.

Pursuing alternative, zero-emission fuels remains our best hope for a healthier future with government recognition and consumer demand spurring investment in solutions. With Tesla leading the charge, the development of battery-powered vehicles has gathered momentum, and electric cars are one of the car industry's biggest growth sectors. Yet beyond battery power, another zero-emission contender is emerging as the greatest potential game-changer.

Hydrogen has been used as a fuel source for many years, powering transport, heavy machinery and spacecraft, but the overwhelming majority of its production has involved input from fossil fuels. More recently, though, a movement towards green hydrogen – produced instead through the electrolysis of water with energy provided by renewable sources – might hold the key to a more sustainable option.

'Our ambition is to provide a zero-emission solution that costs the same as the fuel we're using today,' says Jo Bamford, executive chairman of Oxford-based Ryse, which plans to procure green power for its hydrogen production from offshore wind turbines. He sees hydrogen as a perfect alternative for buses, trains, trucks and shipping, and other heavy vehicles that can be refuelled in a depot. 'It takes five minutes to fill up with hydrogen, it runs for the same distance as diesel and water comes out the exhaust instead of fumes.' It's proving a persuasive argument, with Ryse recently awarded a contract to supply hydrogen to 20 buses in London,

which – when introduced along three bus routes this spring – will become the world's first hydrogen-powered double-deckers.

Bamford is not the only one who recognises the potential. Germany currently runs 12 hydrogen-fuelled trains on its rail network and has placed an order for 42 more, China's government has announced plans to develop fuel stations for hydrogen fuel-cell cars – which sees electric motors powered by a reaction between hydrogen and oxygen, while firms including Toyota, Honda and Hyundai have already brought hydrogen-fuelled cars to our roads. Meanwhile, June 2019 saw the release of an influential report by the International Energy Association (IEA), which prompted the energy agencies of the US, Japan and the EU to pledge future cooperation on hydrogen and fuel-cell technologies. 'This is a critical year for hydrogen,' said Dr Fatih Birol, the IEA's executive director, in its foreword. 'It is enjoying unprecedented momentum and could finally fulfil its long-standing

potential as a clean-energy solution. To seize this opportunity, governments and companies need to be taking ambitious and real-world actions now.'

A number of obstacles currently exist that prevent green hydrogen becoming the industry standard; not least our fixation on battery power – seen as a panacea to our emission crisis by many policymakers. But evidence is mounting that creating adequate infrastructure to support battery-powered vehicles is unrealistic. 'If you want all the cars in the UK to run on battery, between now and 2050 you'll need to add 2,300 charging stations every single day and spend £320bn on upgrading the grid,' says Bamford, referring to findings in a recent report by consultancy Capital Economics. He also highlights the high risks undertaken – often by children – in mining the cobalt necessary for the production of batteries, while a short lifespan means many batteries end up in landfill within a decade of their production.

Another, simpler factor might also be critical if green hydrogen is to save our air quality. 'The most difficult thing to change is human behaviour,' adds Bamford. Currently, green hydrogen costs £6 per kilogram, the same as diesel, and a new report from Hydrogen Council predicts that its cost could fall by up to 60 per cent over the next decade due to the declining costs of renewable electricity generation and increased manufacture of electrolysers. 'A zero-emissions solution will work when it is as easy to fill up with hydrogen as with petrol or diesel, continues Bamford. 'If we can create something that is truly green and that people are willing to change their habits for and use, then we're in business – it's not a ridiculous ambition and I really believe we can do it.'

1. Through electrolysis, hydrogen can be produced using renewable energy and water. When consumed the only output is pure water vapour.

2. The transport sector is the highest carbon emitter in the UK with radical reductions needed to reach net zero emissions by 2050. Hydrogen technology already exists, can be deployed at scale and is the quickest and easiest route to decarbonising transport.

3. Toxic air is a public health emergency and is killing more people in Europe than tobacco smoking. Because hydrogen is more suited to heavier vehicles going longer distances, it can play a significant role in improving air quality in urban areas, delivering health benefits to more people.

4. Hydrogen vehicles can be refuelled in minutes and offer ranges comparable to petrol and diesel equivalents.

SEED OF HOPE

WORDS Spencer Fung - PHOTOGRAPHY Martin Morrell

Ahead of his forthcoming exhibition, Spencer Fung discusses the inspiration behind his work and why nature provides not only his palette but his paints.

In my travels I have seen the scars on the land where ancient forests have been plundered and decimated. From Scotland to Catalonia, Hong Kong to California and as far as Western Australia there's a common theme of loss of woodland for settlement, agriculture and firewood. The majesty of trees and devastation of forests inspires my art. As I feel the pain of the loss I search for a way to readdress our relationship with the land.

I paint nature with nature. I like to be resourceful with local materials, so I gather soil and minerals from cliffs, rocks and forest floors as pigment. I paint with what I can find, in sketchbooks or on paper, or I improvise with rocks, leaves and bark, working the pigment with my fingers and applying it with clumps of moss or leaves.

I began using clay in Dorset. Where the cliffs meet the beach, I came across Jurassic blue clay weathered by time and tide. I love its thickness and elasticity, its colour and texture. The knowledge that it's 120 million years old thrills me. The clay in this series is a biscuit-coloured hue, the colour of Cotswold stone on a late summer day. I dug a chunk of light golden clay with my bare hands and a small trowel and mixed it with blue clay until I reached a palette that retains subtle streaks and tells the story of both.

I tend to choose non-toxic, organic, biodegradable materials. This helps me engage with, and delight in, the natural world. I like the thought that my work is part of a cycle of creation and degradation, leaving no harmful

impact on the environment. The circle and clay series in this exhibition are on recycled cotton rag paper, handmade, using traditional skills, with waste from the garment industry. This creates a soft surface, natural colour and variable texture that suits my work. I like the fact that I am using an upcycled material, and giving discarded fabric a second life.

Sometimes I paint spontaneously in wild places. Other times my work happens after a meditative walk in nature. I pick up fallen natural things, look, see, touch and feel. I digest my thoughts and reflect them later in my sweeping, circular shapes – symbolic of seeds, new birth and the cycle of regeneration. I enjoy the energy flowing through my body when I am creating them, and the feeling of surrendering to nature. Sometimes my circles are one continuous sweeping motion, and occasionally, depending on the soil content, the clay breaks and the circles are connected with different strokes.

In Chinese culture a circle is the symbol of fullness and perfection; I like to think of these works as halos reflecting imperfect perfection. As my collection of seeds from woods and fields grows, I realise I am becoming a naturalist. The variation in shape, form and texture is eye-opening, from futuristic to fluffy, depending on the species and country of origin. Every pine cone or seed pod is intricate and beautiful, each one a unique biodegradable sculpture bursting with reproductive potential. Working with seeds gives me hope for the future. I feel the cycle of life and regeneration, and the power of nature inspires me.

Spencer Fung's exhibition Seed of Hope *runs from 4 to 15 May at Bamford Mayfair in London and from 4 May to 7 June in the Bamford Barn at Daylesford Farm, Kingham in Gloucestershire.*

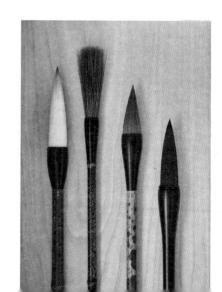

Spring ingredients herald the arrival of a much-anticipated freshness and vibrancy in the kitchen. Pops of colour appear in the garden and hearty winter food gives way to light, colourful dishes. But among the strong favourites at this time of year – the first asparagus, earthy purple sprouting broccoli and sweet summer berries, there are some unsung heroes hiding among the cast of seasonal staples. Often overlooked is the humble but versatile pea. Delicious popped and eaten fresh from their pods, peas bring a subtle sweetness and, if lightly cooked, a welcome bite to spring meals.

A burst of sunshine can bring forth enthusiastic growth in the garden so many of these recipes are devoted to making use of a garden excess or preserving the treasures of the season.

RECIPES Gaven Fuller and Lydia Lishman
PHOTOGRAPHY Lizzie Mayson
FOOD STYLING Frankie Unsworth
PROP STYLING Linda Berlin

Rump of lamb with peas,
broad beans and kale pesto

SERVES 4

160g podded fresh peas
(or use frozen)
160g shelled broad beans
(or use frozen)
250g new potatoes
(such as Jersey Royals),
halved if large
4 rumps of lamb, with skin
(about 160g each)
60g unsalted butter
3 tbsp olive oil
1 banana shallot, finely diced
120ml good-quality
chicken stock
240ml double cream
4 tbsp chopped flat-leaf
parsley
4 tbsp chopped mint
2 Little Gem lettuces,
outer leaves removed,
quartered
sea salt and black pepper

FOR THE KALE PESTO

100g kale
90g pumpkin seeds
280ml olive oil
50g basil
50g purple sprouting
broccoli leaves, cavolo
nero or any other green
you have leftover (or
use more kale or basil)

METHOD

Start by preparing the pesto. Roughly chop the kale and place in a bowl with the pumpkin seeds, then cover with the olive oil. Leave to stand for 5 minutes, then add the basil and your chosen green. Transfer to a blender and blend until smooth.

Blanch the peas in a pan of boiling water for 1 minute and then refresh in iced water. Drain and leave to one side. Blanch the broad beans in a pan of boiling water for 1 minute, refresh in iced water, drain and pop the beans from their skins, then leave to one side.

Bring a large pan of salted water to the boil, add the potatoes and cook until tender, about 15 minutes. Drain and set aside. Once the potatoes are cool enough to handle, peel off their skins.

Heat a large frying pan over a medium heat. Season the lamb with salt and pepper. Allow the butter and olive oil to melt in the frying pan then fry the lamb skin-side down for 8–10 minutes, until golden brown, then turn over and cook for a further 6 minutes. Remove to a plate and allow to rest for 5 minutes.

Add the shallot to the same pan and fry for 2 minutes on a medium heat, before adding the stock, double cream, potatoes, peas and beans. Bring to the boil. Add the parsley and mint and season to taste. Add the Little Gem and simmer for a further 3 minutes.

To serve, thinly slice the lamb. Place two Little Gem wedges in each bowl or plate, spoon over some creamy vegetables and then place the sliced lamb on top and drizzle over a little of the pesto.

Any leftover pesto can be stored in a jar in the fridge, covered with a thin layer of oil, for up to a week, or frozen in ice-cube trays and defrosted as needed.

Chargrilled spring salad

with poached egg

SERVES 2

8 asparagus spears
8 purple sprouting
 broccoli stems
olive oil, for coating
handful of podded peas
2 eggs
sea salt

FOR THE DRESSING

1 tsp Dijon mustard
2 tbsp red wine vinegar
6 tbsp olive oil
1 tsp capers,
 finely chopped

METHOD

Start by whisking together the dressing ingredients in a small bowl and set aside.

Heat a griddle pan over a high heat. Coat the asparagus and broccoli in a little oil and season with salt. Once the griddle is very hot, sear the vegetables for a few minutes, turning frequently, until cooked through and a little charred in places. Remove from the heat and transfer to a bowl. Meanwhile, in a pan of boiling water blanch the podded peas for 1 minute, drain and combine with the asparagus and broccoli.

Bring a separate pan of water to the boil. Turn the heat down to a gentle simmer and gently add the eggs, using ramekins if needed. Cover the pan with a lid, remove from the heat and leave the eggs to poach for 4 minutes.

Drizzle the dressing over the broccoli, asparagus and peas. Serve with the poached eggs on top.

You could swap the poached egg for some crumbled feta or soft goat's cheese. Or, for a plant-based option, replace the egg with a handful of toasted walnuts and/or pumpkin seeds. And if you want to make the salad more substantial, serve it on top of some cooked quinoa or Puy lentils.

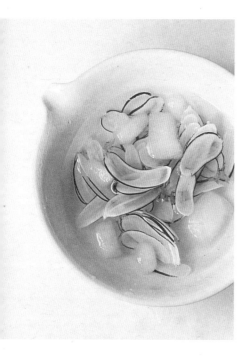

Fregola, radish and pea salad
with lemon and horseradish dressing

SERVES 4

250g podded fresh peas
  (or use frozen)
175g fregola
200g cucumber, peeled,
  seeds removed
  and cut into small dice
25g spring onions,
  thinly sliced
40g flat-leaf parsley,
  roughly chopped
10g mint leaves,
  roughly torn
40g pea shoots,
  roughly chopped,
  plus extra to garnish
35g horseradish cream
130g crème fraîche
25g olive oil
1 tbsp lemon juice
35g radishes, thinly
  sliced lengthways
sea salt and black
  pepper

METHOD

Blanch the peas in salted boiling water for 1 minute, then drain and refresh in cold water, and drain again.

Bring a large pan of salted water to the boil and cook the fregola for 15–17 minutes, or until tender, then drain and transfer to a large bowl. Add the peas, cucumber, spring onion, parsley, mint and pea shoots.

In a separate bowl, mix the horseradish cream with crème fraîche, olive oil, lemon juice and some salt and pepper.

Toss the salad with the dressing, transfer to a serving bowl and garnish with the radishes, extra pea shoots and a drizzle of olive oil.

Despite looking like couscous, fregola is a pasta made in southern parts of Sardinia. Hard durum wheat semolina and water are rubbed together by hand then dried and toasted to produce the small nutty beads. Their surface is ragged and uneven, which makes fregola very good at absorbing flavours. It is both light and substantial – perfect for a spring or summer lunch that will sustain and nourish.

Semi-dried tomato and turmeric hummus
with crostini

MAKES 1 LARGE BOWL

tomatoes, any type
and quantity you
want to preserve
(you'll need a
minimum of 120g
for the hummus)
pinch of herbes
de Provence
icing sugar, to dust

FOR THE CROSTINI
sourdough bread,
very thinly sliced
sea salt and
black pepper
olive oil

FOR THE HUMMUS
1 x 400g tin of
chickpeas, drained
and rinsed
90g semi-dried
tomatoes
juice of 1 lemon
(about 3 tbsp)
3 tbsp tahini
2 garlic cloves,
finely chopped
1 tsp grated ginger
½ tsp grated fresh
turmeric
¼ tsp ground turmeric,
plus more to taste
¼ tsp sea salt,
plus more to taste
pinch of cayenne
pepper (optional)
1–2 tbsp olive oil
or water

TO SERVE (OPTIONAL)
a selection of seasonal
raw vegetables, such
as baby cucumbers,
radishes, baby carrots,
Little Gem lettuce,
cherry tomatoes

METHOD

Line a large roasting tin with a reusable non-stick baking sheet or baking paper. Preheat your oven to 60°C fan.

Start by drying out your tomatoes. Cut them in half then arrange, cut-side up, in the tin. Season with the herbes de Provence and some salt and pepper and dust lightly with icing sugar.

Place in the oven and leave them overnight, or for at least 12 hours. They should be semi-dried and still moist, not dry and tough. Leave to cool completely, then weigh out 90g for the hummus. The remaining tomatoes can be stored in the fridge, covered in oil, for up to 1 week.

To make the crostini, preheat your oven to 180°C fan.

Place the sourdough slices on a baking tray. Very lightly drizzle with olive oil and season with salt and pepper, then cover with another baking tray to weigh them down. Bake in the oven for 12 minutes, or until crisp and golden. The baked crostini can be stored in an airtight container and will keep for up to 1 week.

For the hummus, put the chickpeas, 90g of the semi-dried tomatoes, lemon juice, tahini, garlic, ginger, fresh and ground turmeric, salt and cayenne (if using) into a blender or food processor. Blend on a high speed until creamy and smooth, scraping down the sides as needed. To create a creamier texture, add a bit of oil or water. Taste and adjust the flavour as needed, adding more garlic or ginger, lemon juice, salt or turmeric.

Serve the hummus with the crostini and a selection of seasonal crudités. The hummus can be stored in the fridge for 3–4 days.

A sun-ripened, juicy summer tomato offers a very different experience to the bland, insipid offerings that are made available throughout the year. But as any grower knows, a burst of sunshine can result in a glut.

Drying tomatoes in the oven brings out a rich, sweet flavour and will help you preserve an excess. Toss the semi-dried tomatoes through pasta with olive oil, garlic and basil, or blend them with chickpeas and tahini to make this twist on a classic hummus.

Spiced peach and apricot compote

SERVES 4

6 peaches,
    stoned and quartered
4 apricots,
    stoned and quartered
3 tbsp clear honey
3.5cm piece of ginger,
    finely chopped
3 cardamom pods,
    crushed
100ml water

METHOD

Place all the ingredients in a large saucepan. Heat gently, stirring carefully to combine the flavours. Simmer for 15 minutes, until the fruit has softened. Serve warm, or store in sterilised Kilner jars for up to 1 week.

Preserve soft summer fruits with this fragrant compote that can be served warm or cold. Have it with yoghurt for breakfast, or serve it as a light dessert with cream or ice cream.

Wild garlic and mint pesto

MAKES ABOUT 600G

200g wild garlic leaves
80g mint
90g pumpkin seeds
300ml olive oil

METHOD

Roughly chop the wild garlic leaves and mint. Place in a bowl and add the pumpkin seeds then cover with the olive oil and leave to stand for 5 minutes. Place in food processor and blitz or use a pestle and mortar to pound the mixture until you have a pesto consistency you like – chunky or very smooth.

The pesto can be stored in a jar in the fridge, covered with a thin layer of olive oil, for up to 1 week, or be frozen in in ice-cube trays and used within a month. To defrost, simple heat gently in a large frying pan.

Wild garlic (or ramsons as it is also known) is one of the most easily accessible foragable foods. Come early spring, it carpets wooded areas and shady banks around the UK and is easy to find and identify because the strong scent is so distinctive. If you crush a leaf, you'll know instantly whether you've picked what you were looking for.

It can be used as you would normal garlic, however use it sparingly, as it can be much stronger than garlic cloves. Start with a small handful of chopped leaves to replace a single clove and taste as you go. Making a pesto and freezing it is one of the best and easiest ways to preserve this unique spring delight.

Pea and soft ewe's cheese bruschetta
with wild garlic and mint pesto

SERVES 4

4 x slices sourdough
  bread, about 1cm thick
olive oil
1 garlic clove, peeled
110g podded fresh peas
150g podded
  broad beans
  (you can use frozen)
1 small bunch of mint,
  finely chopped
juice of ½ lemon
75g soft ewe's cheese
about 2 tbsp Wild garlic
  and mint pesto (see
  recipe on page 15)
a handful of pea shoots
sea salt and black
  pepper

METHOD

Heat a griddle pan over a high heat. Preheat your oven to 180°C fan.

Lightly brush one side of each slice of sourdough with olive oil, then gently rub a fresh garlic clove over them. Gently toast the sourdough on the hot griddle on both sides until lightly marked. Transfer the toast to a baking tray and bake in the oven a few minutes until golden and crisp. Remove from the oven and set to one side.

In a bowl, mix the peas, broad beans, mint, lemon juice, a drizzle of olive oil, the cheese and a pinch of salt and pepper.

Pile the mixture on to the four pieces of toast. Drizzle a little of the pesto over the top and add a few pea shoots.

Cranachan
with caramelised spelt flakes

SERVES 4

160g caster sugar
60g spelt flakes
240g raspberries
3 tbsp Drambuie
220ml double cream
1 tsp clear honey

METHOD

Place a frying pan over a medium heat and when hot, add the sugar. Allow it to melt without stirring, then turn up the heat. When it begins to caramelise and turn lovely and golden, mix in the spelt flakes and stir, and leave for about a minute, but don't allow to burn.

Tip the caramel on to a large piece of greaseproof paper and leave to cool. Once it's completely cold and solid, break into pieces then grind into a coarse crumb with a pestle and mortar.

Toss the raspberries in the Drambuie in a small bowl and leave to macerate for a few minutes.

Whip the double cream until soft peaks form, so it's still floppy not stiff. Stir in the honey and half the caramelised spelt pieces.

Take 4 glasses and sprinkle a layer of the remaining caramelised spelt in the bottom of each, then add a layer of raspberry. Cover with the soft cream mixture, then add a few more raspberries. Serve sprinkled with a little of the caramelised spelt on top and a mint leaf, if using.

A cranachan is a traditional Scottish pudding thought to have been created to celebrate the harvest of local raspberries in early summer. It is simple to make and the mixture of lightly whipped cream and fresh seasonal berries bolstered by oats, whisky and a touch of honey rarely fails to please and can look as impressive and elegant or as rustic as you like.

Purists should look away as our recipe strays from the classic – we've replaced the oats with spelt flakes, and have caramelised them in sugar, to give a gentle, sweet crunch. Use jumbo oats to honour tradition. This is a pudding that relies on beautifully soft fragrant raspberries – so make the most of them while you can.

Elderflower parfait
with macerated strawberries

SERVES 8

80ml elderflower cordial
25g caster sugar
4 egg yolks
1 tbsp lemon juice
250ml whipping cream
handful of unsalted
    pistachio nuts,
    roughly chopped,
    plus extra to serve

FOR THE MACERATED STRAWBERRIES

350g strawberries,
    hulled and quartered
1 tbsp elderflower cordial

METHOD

Line a 450g loaf tin with cling film, leaving some overhanging the sides.

Put the elderflower cordial, sugar, egg yolks and lemon juice into a large heatproof bowl set over a pan of gently simmering water and whisk until frothy and thick – this will take about 20 minutes. Remove the bowl from the heat and set aside to cool.

Meanwhile, using a hand-held electric whisk, whip the cream to soft peaks. Fold the cream into the cooled custard mixture, then gently fold through the pistachios. Carefully spoon the mixture into the tin, then fold the excess clingfilm over the surface. Transfer to the freezer and leave overnight.

The next day, place the strawberries in a glass bowl, add the elderflower cordial and gently stir. Leave the strawberries to macerate at room temperature for 1 hour, then chill until ready to serve.

Remove the parfait from the freezer about 15 minutes before you want to serve it to allow it to soften a little. Turn out on to a serving plate and slice, then serve with a spoonful of the strawberries and some chopped pistachios scattered over the top.

Peach and rosemary almond tart
with crème fraîche

SERVES 10

160g unsalted butter
165g caster sugar
160g whole almonds
2 large eggs
20g plain flour
4 large peaches,
    halved
juice of ½ lemon
pinch of chopped
    rosemary
1 tbsp icing sugar
crème fraîche
    or cream, to serve

FOR THE PASTRY

165g unsalted cold
    butter, cut into cubes,
    plus extra for greasing
375g plain flour
165g icing sugar
pinch of salt
5 egg yolks
2 tbsp water
1 egg, beaten with
    a tablespoon of milk,
    for the egg wash

METHOD

Start by making the pastry. In a large mixing bowl, rub the butter cubes into the flour, icing sugar and salt using your fingertips until the mixture resembles breadcrumbs. Add the egg yolks and water and mix just until it forms a dough. Flatten out slightly, then wrap and leave in the fridge to chill for 2 hours.

Grease a 30cm deep fluted tart tin. Remove the chilled pastry from the fridge and leave to soften for 10 minutes then roll it out between two layers of cling film to avoid cracking. Remove the top layer of cling film and carefully transfer the pastry to the tart tin. Press firmly into the corners and then remove the second piece of cling film, leave the pastry edges hanging over the tin and place the tin on a baking tray. Leave in the fridge to chill for 2 hours.

Preheat your oven to 160°C fan. Prick the base of the pastry with a fork then cover with baking paper and fill with baking beans. Blind bake for 20 minutes until light golden brown. Remove the baking beans, reduce the oven temperature to 150°C and continue to bake until golden brown all over, about 10–15 minutes. Brush the inside with the beaten egg wash. Return to the oven for a further 4 minutes to cook the egg wash – this will seal any little cracks in the pastry. Remove from the oven and set aside to cool.

To make the filling, cream the butter and sugar until pale and fluffy. Place the almonds in a food processor or mini chopper and blitz until roughly chopped with some powdered bits and some a little coarser. Stir the almonds into the butter and sugar mixture, then add the eggs one at a time, along with the flour, beating with a wooden spoon, until you have a smooth paste. Place in the fridge for at least 4 hours.

Preheat your oven to 150°C fan. Cut each peach half into thin slices, then mix them with the lemon juice, rosemary and icing sugar.

Spread the almond cream over the baked pastry case, then arrange the peach slices over the top, in concentric circles. Bake in the oven for 60–70 minutes, until golden. Serve warm with crème fraîche or cream.

FEEDING THE MIND

RETHINKING THE GUT-BRAIN AXIS

Keeping our gut healthy is one of the most effective ways
to manage our physical wellbeing. But what is often
overlooked is the significant impact good gut health can have
on our mood and our emotional wellbeing too.

WORDS Rhaya Jordan ILLUSTRATION Paula Troxler

If we feel unmotivated, flat or anxious we might wonder what is wrong with our life. Are we in the right job? Should we reconsider our relationships? A hundred years of Freud has convinced us that any unease in our heads or hearts is a result of an emotional need that is unfulfilled. But science is showing us we may well be wrong, and that the cause of our unhappiness can, in fact, be found in our gut. There is a wisdom to the phrase 'gut feeling'.

The brain and the gut, despite their distance from each other and their dramatically different roles in our body, share a deep connection. In our digestive system a large membrane of nervous tissue, like a thin layer of lace, winds around the length of our intestines. Sometimes referred to as our second brain, this large network of nerves gives our brain constant feedback, even though we may not notice it as such. If an invasive bacteria or a mild food intolerance irritates your gut, your brain will receive a warning that something is wrong. It may not be as evident as you experiencing digestive pain or bloating, it might manifest as mild depression or a sense of unease – a feeling that something is wrong but you don't know what.

We have known that gut bacteria can affect our mental wellbeing for over 100 years. In 1910 an article was published in the *British Journal of Psychiatry* called 'The Treatment of Melancholia with Lactic Bacillus' in which *lactobacillus bulgarus* was shown to be the first 'psychobiotic', a gut bacteria that can impact mental health. And modern research is uncovering many more.

But science is now also clarifying exactly how our gut affects our mood and, more importantly, what we can do about it. It is in fact not our gut that affects mood as such but the health of the billions of bacteria that live inside it – our microbiome, or gut flora. Soon after we are born, our gut lining begins to be populated by billions of bacteria. These bacteria help to keep us healthy, make vitamins for us and as we now know, aid our mental well-being too. In general, the more diverse this population of bacteria is, the healthier we will be.

It is very clear from research with animals how their microbiome affects their mood and behaviour. At University College Cork Professor Ted Dinan and his team took rats who displayed depression – they no longer wanted to play or swim or even hunt for food – and showed that their gut microbiome was altered. When Dinan's team transplanted this 'depressed' microbiome into healthy mice they also began to show depressive features. Astoundingly, changing the mice's gut microbiome made timid breeds of mice adventurous, and adventurous mice more fearful and introverted. Other experiments showed improvements in how easily mice can learn and concentrate.

This work with animals and the effect of their gut flora has been confirmed over and over by scientists around the world, and the link between human mood and the microbiome is just as clear. In one now famous incident, the town of Walkerton in the US had its water supply contaminated with the bacteria *E. coli* and campylobacter in 2000. A year after the tragedy, not only did many of the population have ongoing gut issues but a disproportionate number had developed major depressive illness. Those with serious depression showed high levels of bacterial toxins – called lipopolysaccharides – in their blood. Lipopolysaccharides are small fragments of bacteria that trigger our immune system and are now directly linked to depression.

Our microbiome also produces a surprising amount of neurotransmitters. These are the chemicals that act as messengers in our brain and nervous system and affect our mood, concentration, learning, movement and even feelings of love. The fact that they are made in our gut is probably one of the core reasons a healthy microbiome can contribute to feelings of contentment and wellbeing. For example, there is far more serotonin produced in your gut than you ever will produce in your brain. In your gut, serotonin works as a relaxant, reducing cramping and bloating, but it also sends messages along the nerve which runs directly from your gut to your heart and then on to your brain. It tells the brain that all is well in your gut, helping with that feeling of digestive comfort and of general contentment.

Considering antidepressants are one of the biggest selling categories of drug in the world, isn't it time we took the health of our gut seriously? And what can we do?

We often associate fibre with healthy bowels, but your microbiome also thrives on fibre. In the UK we regularly eat less than half our fibre requirement, starving our gut flora sometimes over years. Eating a wide variety of seasonal fresh vegetables is key to getting your required amount. You don't have to overthink it, even eating your five-a-day will have a positive impact on your microbiota. If you eat fresh food every day, and experiment with new foods you will give your gut all the raw material it needs to grow in health and diversity.

Another thing you can consider is to regularly eat fermented dairy products, such as yoghurt and kefir

or their vegan equivalents. There is direct evidence that regular exposure to the lactobacillus family of bacteria in foods like yoghurt leads to a change in our mood. Fermented vegetables, traditional fermented vinegars, and kombucha and miso are other ways to increase the amount of good bacteria in your diet. There is no perfect time to eat fermented foods, it is more important to find something you enjoy and eat it regularly.

And while probiotic supplements can be all well and good, your main source of good bacteria is the one you already have in your gut. Your population of bifidus, akkermansia, lactobacillus and other protective bacteria explodes when fed properly. Supplements, with a poor diet will not get the job done. Eat more fibre, more vegetables, and experiment with new foods, including some fermented foods, as greater variety will boost your gut flora dramatically.

If you are struggling with mood issues, you may have completely under-estimated how powerful feeding your microbiome can be. A change in mood might be only a glass of kefir away.

Rhaya Jordan is a registered nutritional therapist with over 30 years' experience. She specialises in helping people improve their relationship with food, and works extensively with blood sugar problems and diabetes.

4 QUICK TIPS TO HELP BOOST YOUR GUT HEALTH

1. The natural prebiotics in fibre-rich vegetables and pulses feed the good probiotic bacteria in the gut.

2. Eating fermented foods helps keep your microbiome in optimum condition – choose from yoghurt, fermented drinks like kombucha and kefir, miso, spicy kimchi or sauerkraut.

3. Nurture the gut with organic meat on the bone, slow-cooked cuts and bone broth – they contain the raw materials to heal your gut lining.

4. Balance the gut with the essential oils in ingredients like thyme, rosemary, garlic, chilli, ginger and turmeric – they inhibit bad bacteria.

A TABLE FOR SPRING

PHOTOGRAPHY
Martin Morrell

A gathering
of seasonal
inspiration for
a table setting
that celebrates
the garden
and the
fresh colours
of spring.
Head outdoors
or take the safe
weather option
and opt for a
light-filled space
under cover.

PREVIOUS PAGE: Ludlow white wine glass and white high tumbler; stubby bud vase; Chepstow table knife, table fork, dessert knife and dessert fork; hemp patchwork rug, vintage stoneware vases and vintage terracotta pots; Beatrice bowl 23cm; Beatrice leaf flat plate 29cm, and Lucas bee planter and saucer, all available at Daylesford, various locations

ABOVE: Lucrezia leaf table cloth; Ludlow white wine glass and white high tumbler; Chepstow table knife, table fork, dessert knife and dessert fork; vintage stoneware vases; Lucrezia leaf napkin, Beatrice bowl 23cm; Beatrice leaf flat plate 29cm, and Lucas bee planter and saucer

FAR LEFT: Dining table (from a selection of vintage dining tables available at Daylesford farmshop, Kingham)

LEFT: Lucrezia leaf napkin; Beatrice bowl 23cm and Beatrice leaf flat plate 29cm; hemp patchwork rug

WILDER LAND

WORDS Sebastian Cox
PHOTOGRAPHY Helen Cathcart

Furniture maker Sebastian Cox discusses the reasons behind the publication of his recent manifesto for sustainability, his passion for preserving and protecting English woodlands and how observations of trees help to inform the ethos behind the work at his design studio.

Every spring, we stop production for a week or so and breathe new life into our workshop by tidying, cleaning and making space. As furniture makers, we accumulate lots of jigs, templates and offcuts of British wood that are too beautiful to bin. As we're sending away pallets of scraps to our local college in East London, and tidying the workshop, we're reminded of all the beautiful and meaningful things that have been carried out of our doors to happy customers' homes.

We are also foresters, and our woodland in rural Kent, where I grew up, is undergoing the busiest part of its cycle; rapidly regrowing after our winter's coppicing. Coppicing is a method of woodland management that involves cutting trees at near-to ground level on cycles of around a decade. The hardwood trees, like hazel, chestnut or oak respond by throwing up new, fast-growing stems to reach the light. Our wood has been coppiced since the Norman period and we're continuing that tradition by making contemporary furniture from the trees we cut.

What I find most exciting about this resource is that it provides both humans with materials, and wildlife with habitat. Young plants and new shoots springing into life across the UK's woodland floors

is amplified when larger, older trees are cut down. This sounds odd but makes sense when you consider a calm and shady woodland floor beneath tall trees in full leaf. Without the imposing shade of those taller trees, the cacophony of ground-level life continues. For example, in our woodland in Kent we have foxgloves that lay dormant for 18 years under the soil, beneath old and knotted birch and hornbeam trees (we would call this type of forgotten woodland, 'overstood'). Being a summer-flowering plant, foxgloves don't grow if they lie shaded beneath a closed canopy. Instead, they wait for and thrive off disturbance. When we coppiced our birch to harvest the wood, we cut those overstood trees down, flooding the woodland floor with light. The foxgloves burst from the seed bank, breaking soil and making the most of the newly opened canopy. They have been flowering and seeding since, while the broom, bramble and young

birch trees grow up around them. Along with the foxgloves come more bees and other insects, which bring birds and mammals, and a much longer food chain. Harvesting from our woodland dramatically boosts wildlife; we have (red list) dormice nesting there again thanks to our coppicing.

Of course, there is another benefit to coppicing or woodland management beyond the boost to biological diversity. During their growth, trees are sucking up carbon dioxide from the atmosphere and using it to make structural material so that they can hold their light-hungry leaves closer to the sun; this material is wood. Trees absorb, or sequester, the most carbon dioxide when they are growing, so young, enthusiastic woodland is a very deep carbon sink. As long as we don't burn or rot the wood, that carbon remains out of the atmosphere, making our built and

material environment a huge potential carbon store. Almost every piece of furniture we make has absorbed and contains more carbon dioxide than was emitted in its manufacture. Wood is almost unique as a material for this; we shouldn't think of it as just a familiar material, but a powerful ally in our fight against climate breakdown.

These observations of our woodland have always fed into our thinking as a design studio. I believe that designers have a duty to do good in the world. Every 'bad' object in a landfill site has been designed by somebody, so we must take what we do very seriously. Designers aren't charged with important work like feeding the nation, saving lives, or putting out fires, but I believe, we have a duty, a great collective purpose, to affect positive change, and quickly, and make our material culture more benign.

I spend a lot of time asking myself, what resources does nature want to give us? In attempting to answer this question, as with coppicing, I often look to the past, when we had no choice but to work with nature's rhythms and cycles. I don't look back as a sentimental or romantic indulgence, but as a pragmatic imagination of what our future could look like.

In the last year or so, I've spent (even more time than usual) broadening this question out beyond designed objects, asking, what can our land actually give us? This question, it turns out, is a very big one. We live on an island with limited hectares and greatly depleted wildlife. We rely on many thousands of 'borrowed' hectares of land overseas to feed and clothe us. We also rely on dwindling stores of fossil fuels built up over millennia, using them much faster

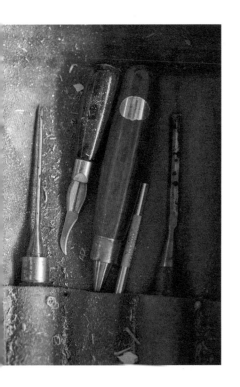

than they could ever be replaced. This is a precarious position to be in when we're causing irreparable damage to the limited resources that we do have on our island. We should strive to become a nation that can obtain our needs from our own area of the earth, and our own period of time.

I have written a manifesto to show that we (the UK) can feed, clothe and supply ourselves with beautiful objects, and meet our energy requirements while making more room for the wildlife that also deserves to live on this island too. It is a proposal for how we can better use our land. I wanted to see if it was possible to use the resources that nature wants to yield; living within our means, without sacrificing a way of life we have

all become accustomed to. Hence its name, *Modern life from wilder land*. It is not a scientific paper and is intended to provoke conversation and suggest what we can ask of our producers, farmers and policy makers; changing demand to drive a change in supply.

I strongly believe that a wilder future, more connected to nature, its natural rhythms and cycles, is a beautiful thing worth aspiring to. I feel more deeply connected to the woodland each time we coppice and see the woodland change with the passing of the seasons. By making a population sensitive to this ebb and flow of nature and its needs we create a society more compelled to act on its behalf and this is a critical change worth making.

'We live in the era of *self*, a culture of "it's
all about you", but that focus on self-identity
has made us lonely.'

HAPPINESS
IS A GROUP EFFORT

WORDS Gelong Thubten
ILLUSTRATION Blandine Pannequin

We humans strive to be happy and to avoid suffering, but many of us are unsure of what happiness is and how to obtain it. We may get what we *think* we want, but we then find ourselves wanting something else; we are never fully content. Perhaps the problem lies in the search – searching leads to more searching – and also in our sense of isolation.

Historically we would think in terms of the wider group – the tribe. Today we live in the era of *self*, a culture of 'it's all about you', but that focus on self-identity has made us lonely. What we fail to recognise is how we are fundamentally interconnected and interdependent: everything depends upon everything else for its existence. Even our ability to breathe relies on the world around us. The trees and plants use sunlight and carbon dioxide to produce the oxygen we inhale. We breathe out, sending out the carbon dioxide that nature needs to produce more oxygen. Our food, clothing and survival depend upon the world around us.

When we don't acknowledge these connections we tend to live from a place of selfishness with its accompanying sense of frustration. To the selfish mind, nothing ever feels good enough or secure enough, making sustainable happiness impossible. The more wrapped up in 'self' we become, the further we stray from genuine happiness, as we get caught up in the endless demands of the ego. If we can learn to respect interdependence, however, a sense of gratitude naturally arises as we see how much we are nurtured by the world around us. Only through cultivating such gratitude can we live in harmony with each other and with our planet.

Sustainable living requires action, but also an examining of our thoughts and attitudes. Just forcing ourselves to want less may not work; what is needed is a revolution in our thinking, whereby we realise that greed does not actually lead to happiness. The material world cannot satisfy us because our desires are limitless, and the world's resources clearly are not. The more we want, *the more we want* – we simply feed a habit, never finding lasting satisfaction. The desire for more things is endless and is encouraged; it causes dissatisfaction rather than happiness and it harms our environment. Greed and levels of consumption have led to a crisis, as has our loss of a sense of community. However, we can protect our environment if we transform our levels of greed. If we can realise that happiness comes from within, we can discover true, *internal* sustainability. By engaging in regular meditation we can connect with our potential for *inner* happiness, realise our own internal resources and reach out to help the world around us. Through transforming our minds we can begin to heal our wounded planet. When meditation helps us find satisfaction within, we will naturally become more aware and careful with our resources. Who owns the world? We all do, equally, and with a positive mind we can learn how to share.

Gelong Thubten is the author of A Monk's Guide to Happiness – Meditation in the 21st Century, *published by Yellow Kite. He is a Buddhist monk who teaches mindfulness meditation in schools, hospitals, companies and other organisations.*

THE COMPLEXITY OF KHADI

INDIA'S HUMBLE TEXTILE

WORDS Malika Verma
PHOTOGRAPHY Prarthna Singh and Gourab Ganguli

For many years India's celebrated handwoven cloth was closely associated with the nation's politics when it became the symbol of Mahatma Gandhi's campaign for independence. Today khadi has found itself at the forefront of a different kind of crusade: its slow production lauded by a global industry that is turning to more sustainable fabrics in an increasing effort to equate consumption with meaning. But the realities of khadi production are complex: changes to its production process have not been adequately communicated to the consumer and the fabric finds itself in a difficult position, albeit one full of opportunity.

If imperfections in a handmade textile indicate perfection, then nothing embodies this more than khadi, India's handspun yarn and handwoven fabric. In simplest terms, cotton, silk or wool are spun and drawn by hand from a spinning wheel called the *desi charkha*, and the resulting yarn is then handwoven on a loom to produce a subtly textured fabric. Learning to spin and weave khadi can be a simple endeavour, but the finesse and complexity of the finished textile will depend on the experience and skill of the weaver.

Supple and slubbed, the delightfully tactile fabric is imbued with cultural, social, economic and political significance. A century ago, Mahatma Gandhi adopted it as a symbol during India's struggle for independence. The act of spinning and weaving the cloth by hand came to represent the pillars of Gandhi's ideology – a society built on self-reliance and self-governance, free from dependence on foreign imports. Bonfires burning mill-made clothing were lit, and India was united across classes with the common ground of nationhood building.

Iconic images of Gandhi spinning the *desi charkha* wearing a khadi *dhoti* (sarong) and shawl are powerful in their simplicity. Whether during imprisonment or while teaching, spinning the wheel for hours was a meditative practice for Gandhi and the image of him at the spinning wheel

remained a constant reminder of self-sustenance, uniting cotton farmers, weavers and wearers across the country.

Decades later, khadi has retained an emotional bond with the public and has also emerged from its humble image to become the cloth of choice for many within India's design community. Innovations include khadi denim and polyvastra, a wrinkle-free weave for the masses. Both are potentially revolutionary in their own right, but the latter is more contentious given that polyester fibre is not sourced from recycled facilities. That is set to change, however, with the introduction of new provisions being opened. Whether making inroads into the £7 billion denim market or addressing issues of affordability and lower maintenance, both innovations highlight khadi's incredible versatility and reach.

But at the crux of this textile's current reality is the unspoken truth that the handspun and handwoven aspect of khadi has largely become semi-mechanised. Introduced in 1955, the *amber charkha* – a semi-mechanised spinning device – allowed spinners to increase their yield and thereby their profits, yet the fabric is still marketed as khadi. Almost the same size as a *desi charkha*, the *amber charkha* has multiple spindles of yarn, and renders the person manning it quite idle, unlike working the *desi charkha* where the yarn is drawn

by hand and the concentration and repetitive motion are believed to instil the process with a meditative aspect. Rta Kapur Chisti, one of India's leading advocates for *desi charkha* khadi, shares technically nuanced differences: 'When the handle of the semi-mechanised charkha is turned, the yarn's twist and thickness is controlled by the pinhole from which the yarn is sucked out; whereas with the traditional spinning wheel, the yarn is being drawn out by hand and therefore its twist and irregularity is determined by the skill of the hand and a softer, supple breathability becomes possible.'

The production of khadi in India is overseen by the government body the Khadi and Village Industries Commission (KVIC). With over 2,000 regional outposts across the country contributing to its production and sales, KVIC has become a brand in its own right, not only selling khadi by the metre but homemade pickles and bottles of shampoo, too. At the moment this cottage industry model is mixed with larger industrial production and requires further aligning; the priority seemingly on increasing revenue at any cost. In an assertion of ownership, KVIC has also been restricting the use of the term 'khadi', silencing brands who use the term publicly in a bid to own the

exclusive title of the nation's cloth. All cloth made by KVIC is produced from a semi-mechanised process and their lack of transparency does not bode well for a textile in dire need of protection and growth.

Sally Holkar is the founder of Women's Weave, a charitable trust based in Maheshwar, Madhya Pradesh. Her organisation is at the forefront of supplying handwoven textiles to the international market and Holkar is one of only a few who explicitly states that her spinners use the *amber charkha*: 'Our textiles are not fully handspun; they're semi-mechanised. However, it's become the norm to define the fabric this way and we do call it "khadi" but we always disclose the process. I am not sure if the retailers do, but for us it's very important not to have misrepresentation. I think we should only look at further definitions if the market demands it and at the moment, our clients don't seem to be requesting them.' The apparent lack of concern indicates a global acceptance of the lowest common denominator – an audience happy to understand just as much is required to make a decision but shies away from a more deeply considered point of view.

Mia Morikawa and Himanshi Shanu, the co-founders of clothing brand

Learning to spin and weave khadi can be a simple endeavour, but the finesse and complexity of the textile will depend on the experience of the weaver

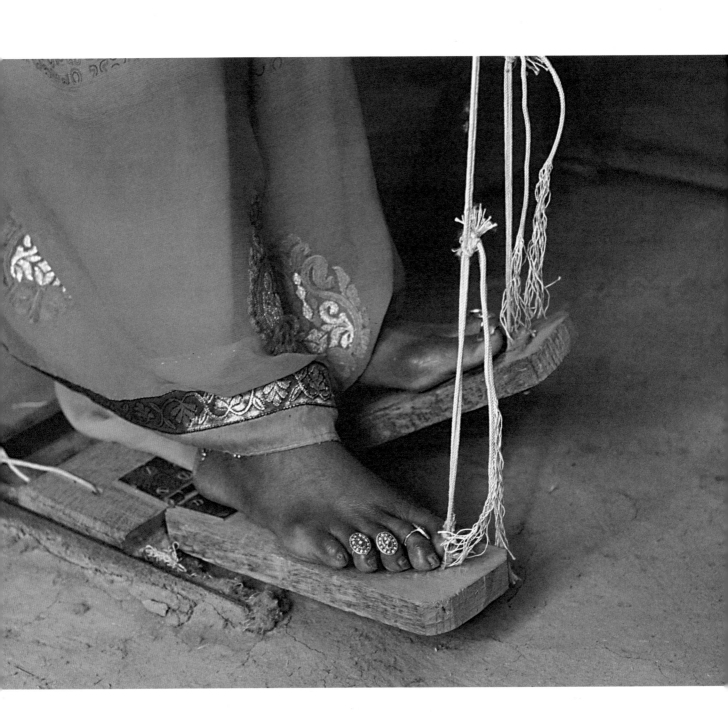

11.11 / eleven eleven, are part of the team involved in the development of khadi denim. They are also deeply concerned about the varying definitions of the khadi craft processes, Shanu echoing that the meditative aspect of handspinning is lost with the *amber charkha*. Unlike the *desi charkha* which engages the hand, body and mind, the other bypasses the need for thought and supports an idle mind, he suggests. Redesigning the *amber charkha* to allow for a more meditative connect while still increasing yields is on their list of things to research inthe future.

'Today, every khadi centre will say that people don't want to do more work that requires extra patience and labour – this is an understandable human sentiment, says Shanu. 'What can increase yield and income, yet engage the mind? How can that be recognised? For example, wine is defined by where and how it has been grown – its terrain and fermentation process – and it becomes a speciality that people know about. When we talk about handspinning no one knows what that means. It is not known because it is not currently formally recognised as a part of our intangible cultural heritage. These are the logistics 11. 11 is trying to understand and share in the simplest way to the end consumer.'

All considered, khadi's profile resonates within the macro trend of sustainable living and requires greater questioning and accountability. For instance, if khadi is sold at retail for the equivalent of £0.75 per yard, what does that translate into as a living wage? With average weaving wages of £1.60 per day, these realities indicate the more pressing need for transparency and standardisation. With inherent complexities of definition, process, production and consumption the future of khadi remains true to the nation it is from: full of potential.

CRAFT IN CONFLICT

WORDS Sophie Richardson
PHOTOGRAPHY Sophia Spring

From the streets of Kabul to the gold mines of Bolivia, ethical jeweller Pippa Small works with vulnerable communities to generate not only jobs but also a sense of pride and identity.

You hear Pippa Small before you see her; each movement sets off a melody of small chimes as clusters of precious stones, shells and small pebbles clash softly against each other.

The strands of multicoloured stones around Pippa's neck and wrists are testimony to a lifetime of travel, each piece imbued with memory, emotion and personal association – a tactile diary of experiences from a life well lived.

Awarded an MBE by the Queen in 2013 for her ethical jewellery and humanitarian work, Pippa has spent the last 20 years travelling the world to work with communities in remote, often war-torn countries, creating beautiful pieces of jewellery that provide a safe, sustainable means of employment for people who previously had little hope.

Along the way she has also designed sustainable jewellery lines for the likes of Tom Ford at Gucci, Christina Kim at Dosa, Bamford and Nicole Farhi, but it is within the colourful cocoon of her Notting Hill store that Pippa seems most at home, surrounded by some of the many gems that she has gathered on her travels over the years.

'I genuinely believe that
the further stretched we are from
creativity, the more we need it.'

Her love of stones stems from early childhood. As a young girl Pippa surrounded herself with rocks and pebbles; sleeping with them, bathing with them and eventually drilling holes in them to create pendants, the better to keep her treasures safe.

As a child she travelled widely with her family, an experience that opened her eyes to different cultures and people, and ignited a fascination for 'otherness' that still guides the designer today.

Her curiosity led to a degree in anthropology followed by a masters in medical anthropology at the School of Oriental and African Studies in London. Soon after graduating she was travelling to Borneo, Thailand and India, working with grassroots organisations to explore ways of protecting indigenous lands, knowledge and biodiversity.

It was on an early trip to Borneo that Pippa noticed the craftsmanship that thrived within tribal communities, with men, women and children all using traditional skills and local materials to create beautiful handicrafts – be it bamboo furniture, gold jewellery or handwoven baskets.

'They had the skills, talent, resources and knowledge to make incredibly beautiful things, but they weren't necessarily making what people wanted to buy,' remembers Pippa. So she began working with the artisans to gently adapt their designs; reimagining traditional skills in a contemporary way, while offering practical commercial advice and access to a wider market that could generate enough sales to ensure a sustainable business model, and so the survival of their craft.

'I realised then that I could make jewellery, which I loved, I could work with artisans, which I also loved, and I could work with different communities from all over the world,' says Pippa. 'It was a really important moment for me and one that completely changed the direction of my life.'

She has since gone on to work with artisans across India, Central and South

America, southern Africa and the Middle East, creating strong, distinctive collections that celebrate each community's traditional skills and techniques.

Pippa's work within these communities is always collaborative. She arrives with a root concept in mind, but the pieces only begin to take shape when she starts to work creatively with the makers, ensuring that their voice and their story is captured. 'Style is inspired by so many things, but fundamentally it's stories,' says Pippa. 'The story of the people who make it, the story of the lands and that they come from, and the histories and the cultures of these ancient civilisations that have been making these extraordinary works for so many years.'

For the last 11 years Pippa's travels have also included regular trips to Afghanistan, thanks to her collaboration with the arts foundation Turquoise Mountain. Established in 2006 by HRH The Prince of Wales and the President of Afghanistan, Hamid Karzai, Turquoise

Mountain was originally founded to protect and promote traditional crafts and cultural heritage in the war-torn capital of Kabul. It has since grown to encompass similar areas of conflict in need of cultural and economic regeneration.

'When you talk about beauty it can seem incredibly superficial, especially in conflict areas,' explains Pippa, 'but what Turquoise Mountain has created is a sanctuary among the tower blocks and tanks and guns and graffiti of Kabul. You enter the foundation and suddenly you feel differently, like you are in a sacred space; the sense of beauty instils a sense of peace and calm and pride.'

As part of her work with Turquoise Mountain, Pippa has established jewellery workshops in the city, providing a safe space for people to come and learn a set of skills that not only provides a consistent means of employment, but also encourages a sense of culture, history and a much-needed feeling of security.

'It's the lack of opportunity that is so marked in places like Afghanistan, where there are no jobs,' says Pippa. 'Obviously, the core thing for people to be able to do is support themselves, but also to have a purpose and a sense of worth – they need jobs, and in the end craft, which I think is so spiritually, emotionally and intellectually fulfilling, can create a tremendous sense of wellbeing.'

Originally it was just men who came to the workshops, but over time Pippa has welcomed a number of women, many of them arriving as shy young girls but soon blossoming into strong, independent women and talented designers in their own right.

'The girls who work in Kabul are so ambitious,' says Pippa. 'They don't just want to be jewellers – they want to be the best jewellers in the world. They want to be seen and heard, and jewellery is their vehicle and vessel to try and reach the world that they can't physically get to.'

Other countries where Pippa collaborates with Turquoise Mountain include Jordan, Bolivia and Myanmar, each offering its own set of stories, skills and indigenous gems for Pippa to weave into her designs.

It is the unique nature of her collections that she thinks people respond well to, recognising the human emotion and experience that underpins each piece. 'I think that without really knowing why, people are beginning to feel a need for something that's a little more individual; in this homogenised world they are seeking something that is very much theirs, happy in the knowledge that no one has anything identical. And I think that increasingly, people are beginning to see these handmade pieces as the ultimate luxury.'

Perhaps even more encouraging is what Pippa calls a resurgence in creativity, with more and more people reconnecting with the act of making itself. She gives the example of a recent Davos forum in which she was invited to participate: 'I arrived thinking it would be about economics; craft is the second biggest earner in Africa and Asia after agriculture, and so I thought it might focus on craft as a development tool.

But that was not the case at all. Instead, what everyone wanted to talk about was how creativity has a vital role in our life and how it impacts us physiologically and spiritually and can be used as a form of meditation.

'I genuinely believe that the further stretched we are from creativity the more we need it. It's seeing its value, appreciating its importance and understanding that we have to protect it.'

It is this passion that continues to propel Pippa from country to country. Next in her sights is Syria, but she is equally committed to cultivating the projects and relationships that she and Turquoise Mountain have worked so hard to foster.

'It's so important not to flit,' says Pippa, and she is understandably proud of the legacy created by Turquoise Mountain in Kabul, where she has watched boys grow into men, bolstered by a safe consistent place of work, and armed with skills that can be passed on to their children. 'It is so fantastic to see,' beams Pippa. 'A secure job is something that gives you hope in such a basic way. And as one friend said to me: nothing stops a bullet faster than a job.'

LET ACTIVISM BE AN ACT OF LOVE

WORDS Satish Kumar
ILLUSTRATION Blandine Pannequin

Countries around the world have declared a 'climate emergency'. From the 93-year-old iconic broadcaster and naturalist Sir David Attenborough to the 17-year-old Swedish activist Greta Thunberg, prominent individuals are passionately reminding the world that the predicament of our precious Planet Earth needs urgent attention.

Behind these high-profile events, millions of ordinary citizens are getting engaged in transforming their own way of life, finding practical solutions to this climate emergency and are themselves enacting environmental policy changes.

In addition to resistance and saying no to the systems that cause climate crisis, people in their millions are also saying yes to a constructive agenda at the grassroots level. They are adopting a low-carbon lifestyle. They are giving up eating meat and rejecting energy-intensive methods of farming and food processing. They are subscribing to companies producing renewable energy, putting solar panels on their roofs and insulating their homes to reduce carbon emissions. They are refusing to shop with a plastic bag or drink water from plastic

bottles and tea from throwaway cups. They are engaged in small or large radical activities and participating in transformative actions in the belief that caring for the climate and looking after our precious planet is everybody's responsibility.

I wholeheartedly endorse and support the actions of school strikers and eco-warriors, but I urge Greta Thunberg and the young and old campaigners to please use the power of love to build the movement for climate care and not be swept away by the force of fear. Let our activism be acts of love. The power of love persuades and transforms, whereas the force of fear frightens and disempowers.

Our actions on behalf of the earth should be acts of love. Ours must be a Love Revolution.

Therefore, we will say no to the policies and practices that harm the earth and cause global heating. And we will also say yes to living simply and sustainably. We will say yes to planting trillions of trees and yes to regenerative agriculture. We will eat healthy, local, organic and nutritious food. We will

support small farmers and growers around the globe. We ourselves will live as artisans and artists. We will support craftsmen and women of the world.

We will never allow despair to diminish our optimism. Activists have to be optimists. Pessimism can lead to journalism but never to activism. With enduring hope and lifelong commitment we undertake the journey of transformation. Yes, activism is a journey and not a destination, it is a long-term process and not a short-term product.

We are all in it together. The economy of waste and pollution, extraction and exploitation, greed and ego have to be brought to an end through the participation of everyone. All of us must join hands and walk together to overcome the perils of pollution and avert the crisis of climate catastrophe. If our mind is polluted by greed, fear and craving then it will give birth to discontentment, consumerism and materialism which will result in the pollution of Planet Earth.

Thus, we do not measure the value of nature in terms of her usefulness

to humans, rather we recognise the intrinsic value of nature and of the entire earth. Nature is not simply a resource for the economy; nature is the source of life itself. Therefore, we must learn to live in harmony with nature, with the Earth and with all living beings.

You may call me an 'idealist'. But what have the realists achieved in the world? The climate crisis is not the work of idealists. It is the activities of the realists that are causing climate crisis, the demise of biodiversity and the pollution of air, water and soil. Under the watch of the so-called realists hunger, wars and many other human tragedies have grown globally. The realists have ruled the world for far too long, and have made a mess of it. Now it is high time to give the idealists a chance, it is high time to listen to Thunberg and Attenborough, to the eco-protestors and eco-pioneers, it is high time to heed re-wilders and agroecologists, school strikers and earth defenders. They are the gentle heroes of our time.

Satish Kumar is the author of Elegant Simplicity *available from resurgence.org/shop and book retailers*

WORDS Jez Taylor - PHOTOGRAPHY Martin Morrell and Matthew Gorman

SWEET PEAS

HOW TO SOW, PLANT AND GROW THESE
SCENTED LATE-SPRING BLOOMS

Even before we started the cutting garden at Daylesford I was aware of the potential for growing sweet peas. Like peas, they thrive in the warm temperatures of late spring, and if you can get them going early you can have yourself a reliable source of sweet-scented cut stems for gifting and cheering up the home all through the summer.

SOW EARLY

Early sowing gives you a great head start. If you can sow in November or December so that you have big bushy plants for planting outside in spring, you can enjoy your first flowers by early June, and if you look after them well enough, with some high potash feed, deadheading and watering, then they can be kept flowering right into September.

PLANTING

Sweet peas don't appreciate root disturbance but they often need to be raised as a transplant so as to protect the seed from hungry mice and from spring frosts. They also prefer a bit of space in order to develop strong root systems. In the garden at Daylesford we sow two seeds per 1-litre pot. When the seedlings are 10cm tall, the weaker one is removed and the remaining one has its tip removed. This has the effect of making the plant throw sideshoots – between four and six. When this growth is no more than 20cm long, transplant the sweet pea into the growing ground, leaving at least 20cm between plants and taking care to plant the root ball with little root disturbance, and into crumbly soil that the roots can easily grow into.

SHELTER AND SUPPORT

Prior to planting in the ground, it is a good idea to set up the structure for them to grow on. A combination of rough string and canes works well, giving the shoots plenty of surface area to cling to. When young, the plants' tendrils aren't particularly strong, so you will need to wind or loosely tie plants on to the structure. Lifting the plant off the soil in this way helps to reduce slug damage, another common problem when establishing sweet peas. Planting in a sheltered position will also encourage the shoots 'up' the framework.

My favourite structure for sweet peas is a wigwam of 2.5m hazel poles with thinner crosspiece branches attached at 30cm intervals. The rustic structures look beautiful – they give immediate height – and when covered in blooms make stunning garden features, wafting sweet scent.

Be warned that plant nurseries and garden centres will often have pots of sweet peas for sale from April which contain up to 20 seedlings in a pot. If you are tempted by these then it really is important to gently separate each seedling from the clump and give it its own pot. Too often people will plant the whole pot and then be incredibly disappointed as the poor plants struggle through close competition to grow even 40cm tall, let alone flower.

If you try to follow my suggestions, you will be delighted by what is probably the most productive cutting flower you will ever grow.

MY FAVOURITES

When choosing which varieties to grow, my selection criteria has generally observed the Daylesford preference for pastel shades, although it is always good to have a few dark types to give contrast. Strong scent and long stem length have been important, although I get less hung up about the length these days as I think it's nice to use stems attached to a bit of leaf and tendril, which gives extra length to use in bouquets.

ANNIVERSARY
has tall stems and an exceptionally long flowering period

BETTY MAIDEN
has delicate blue-edged white flowers with a strong scent

JILLY
is my favourite of the white and varieties starts off cream, maturing to a delicate shade of ivory

HEAVEN SCENT
is a beautiful pale salmon with a rich scent

OUR HARRY
has gently waved lavender flowers with pale edges

Jez Taylor has been managing the market garden at Daylesford farm since 2008.
He grows over 500 varieties of fruit and vegetable organically as well as a range of cut flowers.

CRAFTING FROM NATURE

MAKING NATURAL PLAYDOUGH AND OTHER
SIMPLE PURSUITS TO ENJOY WITH CHILDREN

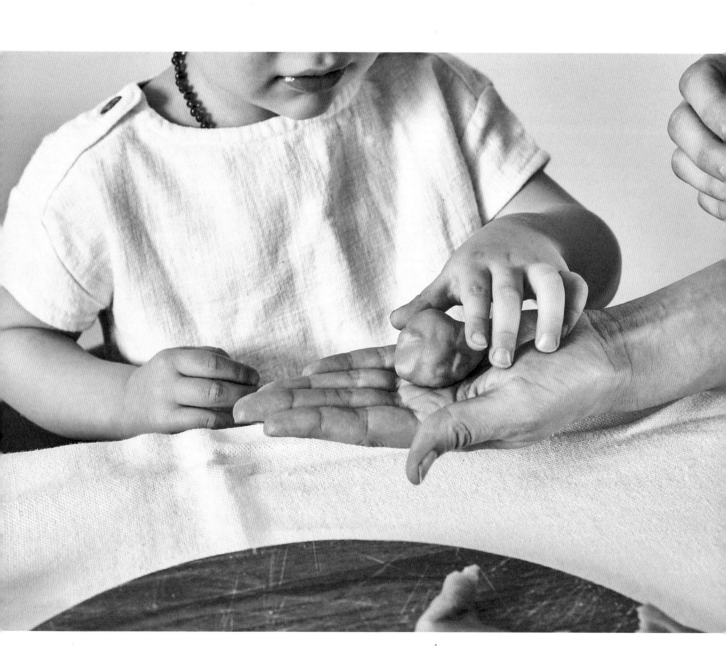

WORDS Leonora Bamford
PHOTOGRAPHY Martin Morrell

When I open our toy cupboard I cringe at the amount of plastic staring back at me. Many are old friends that have been passed down from my eldest to my youngest, yet I still can't help wincing at the sheer mass of it all.

After I got married and had my first child, my mother would often say to me, 'What's wrong with a good old-fashioned book or a stack of building blocks?'. She couldn't understand why I had to fill the children's days with elaborate toys or activity after activity – often my six-month-old would have more of a social life than me, with swimming in the morning followed by baby music and then friends over for a play date.

But with my eldest now in double figures I think that I finally understand. Inevitably the box that a present comes in is far more exciting for any young child, and what is wrong with a simple wooden spoon and a pot to bang it on? This year we've been making lots of crafts and toys at home. Our nanny Anita is like Mary Poppins, and whether it's making wooden craft-stick harmonicas or flip books, we've always got something on the go.

Last year, Pop Up and Play (a wonderful company that develops events for children) helped us keep the children amused at the Daylesford Summer Festival with simple arts and crafts activities, including making natural playdough. What struck me was the simplicity of the crafts and tasks they had on offer and the hordes of little ones wanting to have a go. It wasn't just the toddlers either; we had lots of older children rolling up their sleeves to get involved.

Playdough is one of those things that everyone loves; it's so nostalgic for me and can provide hours of fun for children. We have a tray of homemade playdough at home along with a box of all sorts of buttons, pulses and even feathers, so that we can get really creative making all kinds of objects and creatures. It's easy to store the playdough in glass jars; I normally write the date on the bottom to remind me when we need to make a fresh batch. Although it lasts for a good year, I try and make up a new batch every few months.

What's lovely is that you can scent your playdough using essential oils, and colour it using seasonal ingredients. In summer, raspberries and mint are great but in the winter blackberries will give deeper shades; things like cinnamon, cocoa powder, hibiscus powder and turmeric also add vibrant colour.

Leonora Bamford is the founder of MyBaba.com, an online platform with advice and support for mothers and mothers-to-be.

Another thing we like to do in spring and summer is create nature tables. We will all go out on a long walk armed with nets and a basket and everyone comes home with completely different treasures. We tip everything out on the kitchen table, each with a little area to arrange what we've found. I have lots of old flower books and my mother-in-law gave us a sweet little one about bugs. The children love sifting through their finds and we spend an hour or so drawing and painting, swapping things, and most of all we learn. Even my smallest likes doing rubbings on old scraps of paper with leaves and bits that he's collected along the way. Toys don't have to cost the earth, and making things to do with the whole family can be rather fun too!

TO MAKE
natural playdough

YOU WILL NEED:

125g/1 cup plain flour, plus extra for dusting
140g/½ cup table salt
1 tbsp cream of tartar
1 tablespoon oil
a few essential oils for fragrance,
   such as lavender (optional)

TO COLOUR:

2 handfuls of raspberries, strawberries
   or blackberries, depending on the season
4 tsp matcha powder
4 tsp ground turmeric
4 tsp hibiscus powder
4 tsp cocoa powder

First you need to make your natural dye(s). Place your chosen colour in a pan with 475ml/2 cups water. Bring to the boil then gently simmer for about 20 minutes, until the liquid has reduced to about half. Remove from the heat and leave to cool. Once cool, pour it over a sieve into a jug or glass jar and follow the rest of the playdough recipe.

Put all the dough ingredients, including all the coloured liquid into a pan and mix well. Place the pan on a low-medium heat and stir until the mixture forms a ball.

Remove from the pan and allow it to cool a little, then knead well on a worktop lightly dusted with flour, until the mixture forms a soft, supple dough. Add the essential oil and knead again if you're scenting your dough.

HOW TO ELIMINATE PLASTIC IN THE KITCHEN

WORDS Katriona Jones
PHOTOGRAPHY Lizzie Mayson

1

FOOD SHOPPING

Where and how we shop gives us a real opportunity to reduce our plastic consumption. Try to source loose fruit and vegetables; find your nearest loose-fill store for dry goods, such as cereals, grains and pulses, where you use your own reusable containers. Take your own vessels for meat, fish and cheese bought at counters rather than accepting plastic-wrapped products. Choose retailers that minimise their use of plastic. Of the big supermarkets, for example, Ocado has a 'low plastic' and 'recyclable' section and has stopped using any non-recyclable PVC and polystyrene in its own-label ranges while Sainsbury's has committed to reducing its use of plastic packaging by 50 per cent over the next five years, working with Greenpeace to develop alternatives and to introduce refillable packaging options.

Zero Waste shops are constantly opening. Keep an eye out for one in your local area or visit the website below to find one.
zerowastenearme.com

2

CONSIDER HOW YOUR FOOD IS STORED

Keeping food fresh and well preserved is crucial as we strive to reduce food waste, but consider the materials you use for this. Replace single-use cling film and plastic food bags with naturally made re-usable beeswax wraps or compostable parchment paper.

Choose glass jars, such as Mason or Kilner, over plastic containers – they will last a lifetime and are perfect for dry larder goods, pickles and preserves or fresh soups, stews and stock kept in the fridge. Metal tins and caddies are excellent traditional choices to store bread and baked goods, while linen bags or wicker baskets are ideal for loose vegetables and fruit. Rather than buying new glass or metal containers, try first to re-use the bottles and jars that your food or drinks might have arrived in.
www.beeswaxwraps.co.uk

3

NURTURING THE NEXT GENERATION

Sadly, the vast majority of kitchen items designed for children are made of plastic, with widely available alternatives limited. Step away from the high street and there are sustainable options on the market such as the bamboo fibre cutlery, plates and bowls made by Bamboo Bamboo or stainless steel water beakers, cups and straws which are both hardwearing and long-lasting.

Instead of using plastic bottles and teats for milk, choose glass bottles with biodegradable latex or natural rubber teats available from companies such as NUK or forward-thinking Danish brand Natursutten.

Check that any baby food or children's snacks on your shopping list are packaged in recyclable materials or opt for homemade or loose-fill options, carried in your own sustainably made containers.
www.bamboobamboo.co
www.natursutten.com

4

FOOD ON THE MOVE

Consider using a traditional metal caddie, sturdy glass jar or insulated food canister to transport fresh food. Invest in a reusable sandwich bag rather than relying on cling film or plastic food bags. Swap plastic straws for metal and take cutlery from home rather than picking up single-use plastic forks at the checkout.

For tea, coffee and cold drinks away from home, always use your own reusable cup or bottle – this is a fast way to reduce single-use plastic consumption every day. Choose vessels made from sustainable, durable materials that are free from harmful chemicals, such as those made by Klean Kanteen, which come with a lifetime guarantee.
www.kleankanteen.co.uk

When it comes to plastic, the outlook for our planet is bleak. Globally we produce 300 million tons of plastic each year, with half of this designed for single use, the most damaging kind. If our consumption of these harmful plastics continues at its current rate, by the middle of this century our oceans may contain more plastic than marine life.

However, we can make a difference. For many of us, the kitchen is the part of our home where we are surrounded by unnecessary plastic, from the worst kinds of single-use packaging to toxic cleaning products and cheap tools or appliances. By considering what we bring into our kitchens, how those items are packaged and the impact they might have on our planet, we can choose to make simple swaps, opting for sustainably-made, environmentally-friendly alternatives.

The good news is that as awareness of plastic pollution grows, innovative choices and solutions are becoming available. There has never been a more prescient time to tackle plastic use, and no better place to start than our own kitchens. Although completely eradicating plastic at home is no easy task, small changes are better than none – simply addressing our consumption of single-use plastics can make a big difference.

5
CLEAN CONSCIOUSLY

The vast majority of household cleaning products are made from, or packaged in, plastic and also contain chemicals harmful to our waterways and oceans.

Choose cleaning sponges and scourers made from natural materials; invest in good quality wooden washing up brushes with natural fibre bristles; use organic cotton cleaning cloths and go for bamboo fibre reusable kitchen towels such as those made by Ecoegg.com.

Try to use environmentally-friendly cleaning and laundry products, such as soap nuts, which contain saponin, a naturally occurring detergent and check that any packaging on products you buy is recyclable or biodegradable. If possible use, your own glass spray bottle dispensers at home, refilling as needed from your nearest self-fill retailer.
www.Ecoegg.com

6
PREPARATION AND COOKERY

Buy wisely when shopping for kitchen utensils, picking good-quality items designed to last a lifetime. Look for well-made kitchen knives with wooden handles; durable metal pots and pans without polymer-based non-stick coatings; wooden chopping boards, spoons and mixing bowls rather than plastic, and glass-lidded bowls such as Pyrex for cookery and food storage. Traditional enamel baking tins and trays are a better choice than cheap non-stick versions and always choose metal sieves, colanders, measuring cups and scales.

7
APPLIANCES

Even the most environmentally-friendly electric kitchen appliances are made with some plastic components, so look for kettles, toasters or blenders made by companies with green credentials, who minimise their use of harmful plastics and offer a lifetime guarantee on their products. We love Dualit toasters – each assembled by hand and made from completely replaceable, repairable parts.

Consider a classic stovetop kettle, made from steel or aluminium and when replacing your oven or hob think about eco-friendly or reconditioned range cookers, which use minimal plastic. Rather than throwing away appliances, investigate whether they can be repaired or reconditioned and if not, ensure they are recycled or disposed of properly. Above all, avoid cheap, replaceable plastic appliances which cause harm to the planet both during production and at the end of their life.
www.dualit.com

8
RECYCLE, REUSE AND REPAIR

Even the most conscientious are likely to find a little plastic creeping into their kitchens – make sure to dispose of it correctly, checking the labels on packaged food products, packets and bottles. Speak to your local recycling centre or council to find out what you can recycle, where and how. Use biodegradable plant-based bin liners instead of black plastic sacks and before you throw something away, first ask yourself if it could be reused or rehomed.

TREAD SOFTLY

WALKING KENYA'S ANCIENT PATHS WITHOUT LEAVING A TRACE

WORDS Alice B-B
PHOTOGRAPHY Helen Dufresne and Alice B-B

The Kenyan sky is velvet-black bar a smattering of stars when I hear my alarm. But unlike my London wake-up call, there is no strident iPhone or buzzing clock; instead it's the magical singing voice of Lemagas, a Samburu tribal warrior, who approaches my mosquito-netted tent with a bucket of water for me to wash my face and brush my teeth, ready for the day's adventure in the African bush.

Kenya is the place where I feel most alive, but I'm all too aware that this is a testing time for wanderlust: I'm increasingly wracked with carbon guilt, aware of hotels and resorts telegraphing their often meretricious greenwashing, and I can't help question the argument that travelling halfway around the world to take pictures of animals helps the conservation battle. Terrifyingly, I recently learned that if tourism were a country, it would be the fourth largest emitter of carbon in the world.

However, a walking camel safari with Remote n Wild in northern Kenya is, I believe, the closest I can get to a guilt-free fix of the travel drug I so crave. I'm here with my family, dropped off by propeller plane on to a small bumpy runway amid acacia trees in the middle of nowhere. No Wi-Fi, no phone connection; we're totally off-grid in Samburu country. Our welcome party is a caravan of 50 camels, a gang of noble, beaded Samburu warriors, and our leaders, Helen Dufresne and Pete Ilsley. Not forgetting Salau, their trusty Rhodesian ridgeback, always at the ready for a scrap with a lion.

Luggage strapped to the camels, we head off into the wilds, as our warrior protectors sing to the beat of wooden camel bells. Austere beneath the harsh sun, the bush is somehow home to wild animals and indigenous people. The rhythm of the journey is beautiful in its simplicity. We cover miles on foot each day, starting before dawn while it's cool and stopping for a mid-morning feast; a breakfast of fruit, freshly-baked bread, eggs and bacon cooked beneath an acacia tree. Well fed, we set off again, down *luggas* (dried-up river beds), through dense forest or traversing high mountains.

We travel with minimum impact, leaving barely a trace. Tents packed up, the long drop loo, framed by a portable mahogany thunderbox, is filled in; not a scrap of rubbish is left behind. We use no electricity: our evening shower is a sack of foraged water heated over a fire and suspended in a tree, taken with breathtaking views over the vast, wild landscape.

And we travel with positive impact: we happen upon a family of baby warthogs suffering due to the drought, so we open up a nearby waterhole to give these thirsty little lives a chance. We meet a farmer who has lost a cow and help him to find it. We come across a man whose testicle has swollen to the size of a melon; medical help is delivered by Pete. And on our journey we visit the work of the Milgis Trust, a foundation set up by Helen and Pete to conserve this precious ecosystem – a thriving school, anti-poaching rangers and solar-powered water projects.

We mindfully travel a version of the Samburu's nomadic way, walking ancient paths cooled by ancient winds. We slow right down, appreciative of nature, life, the planet. Luxury is recalibrated: after six days in the bush, Pete still manages to produce an ice cube for a gin and tonic – it's better than any diamond. And after dinner, we tell stories round the camp fire while watching shooting stars, before heading to a mattress beneath a mosquito net for a more beautiful, dreamy sleep than in any swanky five-star hotel. And all the while, my conscience is clear... knowing that we're treading softly.

Remotenwild.com
Milgistrust.com

CARBON FARMING TO REVERSE CLIMATE CHANGE

WORDS Craig Sams
ILLUSTRATION Hugo Guinness

The world's soil is its single most valuable commodity yet we pillage its nutrients, desolate its health and overlook its potential to help solve one of the biggest crises facing humanity. How can we transform the damage we have caused and make use of the one resource that could help us stop the planet warming?

In the 1970s my family and I published a magazine called *Seed: The Journal of Organic Living*. At that time we were already concerned about climate change: we still took fields and forests for granted; the onslaught of industrial agriculture was just beginning to take effect; and we were heartened by the fact that the insecticide DDT had been banned, little realising that it would be replaced by a multiplicity of other carcinogens. We knew that organic food was the future, but as my brother Gregory, editor of the magazine, commented: 'We could see the future but we were looking through the wrong end of the telescope – it all turned out to be much further away than we thought.' Today, climate change is accepted as an emergency: the planet is warming and we are losing the race to save all the inestimable physical wealth and cultural value that humankind created over the centuries, and yet we have singularly failed to use the most efficient tool for reducing carbon dioxide levels: photosynthesis.

Nothing else comes close to sucking carbon out of the atmosphere, yet we neglect it. Two decades of policies to address the rising threat of catastrophic climate change have focused on reducing emissions. They failed, however, to slow the increase in greenhouse gas levels. Instead, directly and by default, government policies have brought about continuing increases instead.

Forestry and farming are the cheapest and most effective ways to take carbon out of the atmosphere, sequestering it in the vast unexploited reservoir of the soil and trees. Yet instead of actively pursuing these low-cost options we have deforested and degraded forest carbon and soil sinks. How can we fix this?

The '4 per 1000' ('Quatre pour Mille') initiative launched at the Paris COP21 in 2015 aims to do just that, by rewarding carbon farming. '4 per 1000' states that, if farming and forestry increased soil organic carbon (a measurable component of soil organic matter) annually by four parts per thousand, that would be enough to totally offset the 16-billion-tonne annual increase in greenhouse gas levels. With carbon a marketable crop, we could stop worrying about global warming.

The '4 per 1000' initiative is predicated on there being a price on carbon, whether emitted into the atmosphere or removed from the atmosphere. The government would set a price for carbon and all emissions of CO_2 would be paid as part of a company's tax bill, declared as part of its annual returns. If a company could purchase carbon offsets for less it could deduct these offsets from its tax bill from carbon-aware farmers.

Soil is the world's most important and valuable commodity. With a realistic carbon price, we would not suffer the resource misallocation of agricultural subsidies such as in the Common Agricultural Policy (CAP). Wind and solar power are getting cheaper, but they are nowhere near as competitive as 4/1000. Forests, pasture and arable farmland can easily sequester '4 per 1000 per annum'. Yet globally we still lose 31 football fields per minute of productive agricultural land because industrial farming methods take no account of carbon emissions.

How does a carbon price affect fossil fuel prices?

There is a financial opportunity. The government simply establishes a tax that can be offset by carbon credits. This then puts carbon dioxide, like any other valuable commodity, in the hands of markets.

Fossil fuel emissions amount to 33 billion tonnes of CO_2 a year globally. At £50/tonne, the market for carbon credits would be more than £1.5 trillion. If Britain leads on this by example then London would be the

financial hub for carbon trading. The City of London has the depth of liquidity and the reputation for integrity that a global carbon market will need to succeed.

The flow of cash into sequestration would be transformative. Agricultural subsidies could fall away without impacting on land values. Rural economies would be invigorated and farming could begin to remediate the misallocation of resources that current CAP policy encourages.

What is the scale of the opportunity? Carbon sinks are primarily forests, fields and meadows.

The world has 1.5 billion hectares of arable land, 4 billion hectares of forest and woodland and 5 billion hectares of grassland, a total of 10.5 billion hectares that can be put to work removing CO_2 from the atmosphere. The annual net increase in CO_2 levels is 16 billion tonnes. If every hectare of our available land annually removed 4 tonnes of CO_2 then we would remove 41 tonnes of CO_2 from the atmosphere every year, which would get us back to pre-industrial levels in just 35 years.

Soil is the foundation of our natural capital. In a capitalist system it should be valued. Farmers could insure against loss of carbon. Banks would advance loans against land to

farmers who operate best practice carbon farming in the knowledge that the asset that is loaned against is increasing in value as its carbon content increases.

The cost of low carbon food (organic) would come down and the cost of high carbon industrial food would go up. No longer would price be a barrier to eating food that is rich in nutrients, low in pesticide residues and delivers tangential social and environmental benefits.

Carbon sequestration in farmland, pasture and forests is a cheap and effective way of reducing greenhouse gas levels. Compliance with agreed Paris COP21 targets will be unlikely if we continue to depend on technological solutions and biofuels to reduce emissions. Using up precious soil and forests for the production of biofuels is wasteful, uneconomic and does nothing to help mitigate climate change. An economic incentive to maximise soil and forest sequestration of carbon dioxide is the most effective, practical and low-cost solution to achieving greenhouse gas reduction. Britain has the chance, at the COP26 in Glasgow in November, to set the world on the track to sanity and survival.

Let's hope that we can take rational and urgent actions to turn things around while there is still time.

WHAT WOULD HAPPEN IF THERE WERE A £50 PER TONNE CO2 PRICE?

Farmers would increase soil carbon by the use of grass leys (a piece of grass put down for a single season or a limited number of years) and compost. They would minimise tillage and grow green manures to keep ground cover all year round.

Nitrates, pesticides and herbicides would become uneconomic in many applications and farmers would minimise or abandon these inputs.

Carbon from straw, sawmill waste and forestry arisings would be converted into biochar (agricultural charcoal) then added to the soil to permanently enhance fertility and increase the carbon in the soil 'carbon bank'. Biochar is 80–90 per cent pure carbon and stays in the soil for centuries.

Farmers would plant trees and hedgerows instead of growing rapeseed for biodiesel.

Craig Sams is the co-founder and executive chairman of Carbon Gold Ltd, a carbon sequestration business based on the use of biochar as a soil improver. Biochar is emerging as a major tool for mitigating climate change and restoring our planet's degraded soils. He is a former chairman of the Soil Association and co-founder of the award-wining Green & Black's organic chocolate.

Wood burning would end overnight. Britain's Drax power station in Yorkshire burns wood pellets made by clearing 1.5 million hectares of forest in the US and Canada every year. That's as much as the annual loss of Amazon rainforest. It has to stop.

Wood would replace steel and concrete in buildings and homes. Wood is carbon negative (it removes carbon from the atmosphere).

The £1.5 billion government subsidy to date wasted on carbon capture and storage research would be saved.

Peat use would end overnight – peat bogs capture more carbon than any land use other than salt marshes.

The sea would be more productive. Reduced fertiliser use and reversal of soil erosion would herald the end of harmful algal blooms that damage coastal ecosystems and fish stock populations.

The Presence of Trees

I have always felt the living presence
of trees
the forest that calls to me as deeply
as I breathe,
as though the woods were marrow of my bone
as though
I myself were tree, a breathing, reaching
arc of the larger canopy
beside a brook bubbling to foam
like the one
deep in these woods,
that calls
that whispers home.

– Michael S. Glaser